CATHOLIC PRAYER BOOK FOR CHILDREN

CATHOLIC PRAYER BOOK FOR CHILDREN

EDITED BY JULIANNE M. WILL
ILLUSTRATED BY KEVIN DAVIDSON

Our Sunday Visitor Publishing Division
Our Sunday Visitor, Inc.
Huntington, Indiana 46750

Nihil Obstat
Rev. Michael Heintz
Censor Librorum

Imprimatur
✠ John M. D'Arcy, Bishop of Fort Wayne-South Bend
November 3, 2003

Our Sunday Visitor Publishing Division
Our Sunday Visitor, Inc.
200 Noll Plaza
Huntington, IN 46750

Hardcover edition, ISBN: 1-59276-046-5 (Inventory No. R97)
Paper edition, ISBN: 1-59276-047-3 (Inventory No. R98)

Cover design by Kevin Davidson
Interior design by Rebecca Heaston
Original prayers by Julianne Will

Printed in Canada

To my darling Mia, the inspiration for and answer to so many of my prayers.

TABLE OF CONTENTS

INTRODUCTION

Children so often take a solemn approach to prayer. It must be said with bowed head and folded hands, they say. Or recited at night. Formal prayers are always best, they believe, though you can ask God for something, too ... maybe to help someone who is sick feel better.

The traditional prayers of our Catholic faith are beautiful treasures. They offer children the blessings of routine, ritual, stability, and a sense of belonging, a Catholic identity. They are familiar and unchanging.

One of my goals for the children who read this book is to illuminate the meaning of our traditional prayers. The stories behind each can capture a young and active imagination and breathe life into the lines a child memorizes. Children will recite and take comfort in the prayers common to our faith throughout their lives. How much more spiritual those prayers can be when thought or articulated knowing the powerful feelings that inspired the authors.

What often surprises children more is the notion that a new prayer or one of their own composition can be equally effective and equally important to God. Prayer can be relevant, current, and specific. It can be made up, sung, danced, lived, or whispered. It can go beyond asking God for favors and include praise, joy, thanks, or the deepest fears.

Children are bound by rules in so many areas of their lives. But there is no wrong way to pray. Talking – and listening – to God can incorporate the formal and the free-spirited with one simple guiding principle: Pray often.

I wish parents, teachers, instructors, and family members great joy in helping children develop the most powerful and loving relationship of their lives. And it is with great enthusiasm that I present to children these means of growing closer to God.

– Julianne Will

God listens when you pray, and he rushes to you when you are crying or hurt or sad. God will never hurt you. I love to pray, and you will, too.

– Mia Stephenson

PRAYERS ALL CATHOLICS SHARE

Basic Prayers of the Catholic Faith

SIGN OF THE CROSS

In the name of the Father,
and of the Son,
and of the Holy Spirit.
Amen.

OUR FATHER

Our Father,
who art in heaven,
hallowed be thy name.
Thy kingdom come,
thy will be done
on earth as it is in heaven.
Give us this day our daily bread,
and forgive us our trespasses,
as we forgive those who trespass against us;
and lead us not into temptation,
but deliver us from evil.
Amen.

When the apostles asked Jesus how they should pray, he gave them the words of the Our Father. Read about it in Matthew 6:9-13.

Hail Mary

Hail Mary, full of grace.
The Lord is with thee.
Blessed art thou among women
and blessed is the fruit of thy womb, Jesus.
Holy Mary, Mother of God,
pray for us sinners,
now and at the hour of our death.
Amen.

*The Hail Mary uses the same words the angel Gabriel said
when he told Mary she would be Jesus' mother. This prayer
also includes the words Mary's cousin Elizabeth said when
Mary visited Elizabeth. Read about it in Luke 1:28, 42.*

Glory Be (Also called the Doxology)

Glory be to the Father,
and to the Son,
and to the Holy Spirit.
As it was in the beginning,
is now, and ever shall be,
world without end.
Amen.

APOSTLES' CREED

I believe in God, the Father almighty,
   creator of heaven and earth.

I believe in Jesus Christ, his only Son, our Lord.
   He was conceived by the power of the Holy Spirit
      and born of the Virgin Mary.
   He suffered under Pontius Pilate,
      was crucified, died, and was buried.
   He descended to the dead.
      On the third day he rose again.
   He ascended into heaven,
      and is seated at the right hand of the Father.
   He will come again to judge the living and the dead.

I believe in the Holy Spirit,
   the holy catholic Church,
   the communion of saints,
   the forgiveness of sins,
   the resurrection of the body,
   and the life everlasting. Amen.

*The Apostles' Creed and the Nicene Creed list the things
Catholics believe. We say the Nicene Creed, found on page
60, during Mass each week.*

ACT OF FAITH

O my God, I firmly believe that you are one God in three
   divine persons,
the Father, the Son, and the Holy Spirit.
I believe in Jesus Christ, your Son,
who became man and died for our sins,
and who will come again to judge the living and the dead.
I believe these and all the truths that the holy Catholic
   Church teaches,
because you have revealed them,
who can neither deceive nor be deceived.
Lord, increase my faith.
Amen.

ACT OF HOPE

O my God, trusting in your infinite goodness
   and promises,
I hope to obtain pardon of my sins,
the help of your grace, and life everlasting,
through the merits of Jesus Christ, my Lord
   and Redeemer.
Lord, may I live with you forever and ever.
Amen.

ACT OF LOVE

O my God, I love you above all things, with my whole
   heart and soul,
because you are all-good and worthy of all my love.
I love my neighbor as myself for love of you.
I forgive all who have injured me, and I ask pardon
   of all whom I have injured.
Lord, may I love you more and more.
Amen.

II.

ON A WING
AND A PRAYER

Prayers to Angels

Guardian Angel

Angel of God, my guardian dear,
to whom God's love commits me here,
ever this day, be at my side,
to light, to guard, to rule and guide.
Amen.

Prayer to Saint Gabriel, the Archangel

O God,
who from among all your angels
chose the archangel Gabriel
to announce the mystery of the Incarnation,
mercifully grant that we,
who solemnly remember him on earth
may feel the benefits of his patronage in heaven,
you who live and reign forever and ever.
Amen.

In Your Arms

Beautiful angel, loving protector,
hold me close in the fold of your arms.
Surround me with your warm embrace,
keeping away all fear and harm.
Sent by God to give me peace,
you bring his light to ease my fright.
Hold me close and help me sleep,
dear angel, be with me through the night.
Amen.

III.

SAINTS, LEND ME YOUR EARS!

Prayers to the Saints in Heaven

PRAYER TO SAINT ANTHONY

O Holy St. Anthony, gentlest of saints, your love for God and charity for his creatures made you worthy, when on earth, to possess miraculous powers. Miracles waited on your word, which you were ever ready to speak for those in trouble or anxiety. Encouraged by this thought, I implore of you to obtain for me *(request)*. The answer to my prayer may require a miracle; even so, you are the saint of miracles. O gentle and loving St. Anthony, whose heart was ever full of human sympathy, whisper my petition into the ears of the sweet Infant Jesus, who loved to be folded in your arms; and the gratitude of my heart will ever be yours.

Amen.

Saint Anthony of Padua (1195-1231) is called a Doctor of the Church, meaning he is honored for his writing and teaching and for his holiness. Anthony was a member of the Franciscan Order of religious men and women and was known for working miracles. He is the patron saint of finding lost items.

BREASTPLATE OF SAINT PATRICK

Christ, be with me,
Christ within me,
Christ before me,
Christ behind me,
Christ be on my right,
Christ be on my left,
Christ where I lie,
Christ where I sit,
Christ where I arise,
Christ beneath me,
Christ above me,
Christ in the hearts of all who love me,
Christ in quiet,
Christ in danger,
Christ in the mouth of friend and stranger.
Amen.

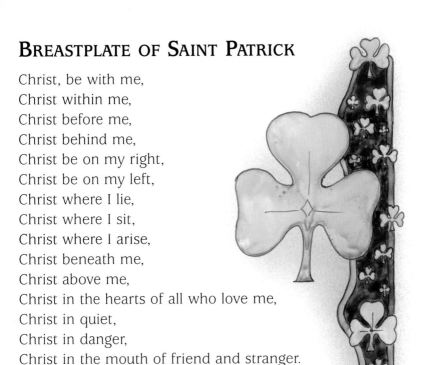

This prayer is ascribed to Saint Patrick (385-461), the patron saint of Ireland. Born in Britain, he was captured when he was sixteen and made a slave in Ireland. Patrick escaped six years later, but felt called to return to preach. As a missionary bishop, he was very popular and converted most of the Irish people to Christianity.

PRAYER TO SAINT THÉRÈSE OF LISIEUX

Dearest Saint Thérèse,
When you were small, you were like us all:
You played and pouted, laughed and shouted.

But your life grew more holy day by day,
When you did good deeds in your Little Way.

I pray to you to help me bring
God's love when I do anything.
Amen.

*Saint Thérèse (1873-1897) was born in France, the youngest
of nine children, and followed her sisters to the Carmelite
convent when she was just fifteen. Saint Thérèse was known
for turning everything, even chores, into prayers; this was
her famous "Little Way." She died at age twenty-four and is
now a Doctor of the Church.*

PRAYER OF SAINT FRANCIS OF ASSISI

Lord, make me an instrument of your peace.
Where there is hatred, let me sow love;
where there is injury, pardon;
where there is doubt, faith;
where there is darkness, light;
and where there is sadness, joy.
O, Divine Master,
grant that I may not so much seek to be consoled,
    as to console;
to be understood, as to understand;
    to be loved, as to love.
For it is in giving that we receive;
it is in pardoning that we are pardoned;
and it is in dying that we are born into eternal life.

This prayer is ascribed to Saint Francis (1181-1226). He grew up in a rich family in Italy, but as an adult he gave away all he had to care for the poor and started the Franciscan Order for religious life. He is also known for making the first Christmas Nativity scene, for caring for birds and animals, and for receiving the stigmata, the marks of Jesus' crucifixion, on his hands and feet.

Prayer to Saint Joseph

O Saint Joseph, whose protection is so great, so strong, so prompt before the throne of God, I place in you all my interests and desires. O Saint Joseph, do assist me by your powerful intercession and obtain for me from your Divine Son all spiritual blessings through Jesus Christ, Our Lord; so that having engaged here below your heavenly power I may offer my thanksgiving and homage to the most loving of fathers. O Saint Joseph, I never weary contemplating you and Jesus asleep in your arms. I dare not approach while he reposes near your heart. Press him in my name and kiss his fine head for me, and ask him to return the kiss when I draw my dying breath. Saint Joseph, patron of departing souls, pray for us. Amen.

Saint Joseph (first century) is honored as the husband of Mary and foster father of Jesus. He was a carpenter known as a fair and honest man.

The Incarnation, by Saint Augustine

Maker of the sun,
he is made under the sun.
In the Father he remains,
from his mother he goes forth.
Creator of heaven and earth,
he was born on earth under heaven.
Unspeakably wise,
he is wisely speechless.
Filling the world,
he lies in a manger.
Ruler of the stars,
he nurses at his mother's bosom.
He is both great in the nature of God,
and small in the form of a servant.

Saint Augustine of Hippo (d. 430) is a Doctor of the Church and one of the Church Fathers. After living a wild life as a young man, he converted to Christianity with the prayers and encouragement of his mother, Saint Monica, and his teacher, Saint Ambrose. Augustine is known for his powerful preaching and writing; his work is still read and used today.

Prayer to Help Me Be a Saint

The saints were really amazing, God;
   their love for you was great.
They prayed and preached and spread your word,
   even when faced with hate.
Helping, sharing, spreading grace,
   they'd give up their last dime.
Now they're blessed with the joy of heaven
   until the end of time.

But the saints were still just people, too;
   they sometimes did things wrong.
They doubted, worried, and sinned at times,
   and didn't always get along.
So maybe there's still hope for me,
   to be named a saint, too.
Lord give me strength to try again,
   so I can live with you.
Amen.

I Have a Mom in Heaven, Too

Marian Prayers

THE MEMORARE

Remember, O most gracious Virgin Mary,
that never was it known that anyone who fled
    to thy protection,
implored thy help, or sought thine intercession
    was left unaided.
Inspired by this confidence, I turn to thee,
    O Virgin of Virgins, my Mother.
To thee I come, before thee I stand, sinful and sorrowful.
O Mother of the Word Incarnate,
    despise not my petitions,
but in thy mercy hear and answer me.
Amen.

THE ROSARY

First make the Sign of the Cross. *(see p. 12)*

Then pray the Apostles' Creed while holding the crucifix.
(see p. 14)

Pray the Our Father on the first bead. *(see p. 12)*

Pray the Hail Mary on each of the next three beads.
(see p. 13)

Pray the Glory Be. *(see p. 13)*

On the next bead, read and think about the first of that
day's mysteries, then pray the Our Father.

Pray the Hail Mary on each of the next ten beads. Each
set of ten beads is called a "decade."

Pray the Glory Be.

On the next bead, read and think about the next of that
day's mysteries, then pray the Our Father.

Continue with ten Hail Marys, the Glory Be, the mystery
and the Our Father until you have finished all five
decades.

When you are finished, pray the traditional closing
prayer, the Hail, Holy Queen. *(see p. 31)*

The Joyful Mysteries – prayed on Mondays and Saturdays

The annunciation of the Lord: The angel Gabriel tells
Mary she will have a son named Jesus.

The visitation: Mary goes to see her cousin Elizabeth,
who is having a baby, too.

The nativity of the Lord: Jesus is born.

The presentation of the Lord: Baby Jesus is taken to
the temple.

The finding in the temple: Jesus is lost; Mary and
Joseph discover him preaching.

The Sorrowful Mysteries – prayed on Tuesdays and Fridays

The agony in the garden: Jesus prays about dying on the cross.

The scourging: Jesus is beaten.

The crowning with thorns: The officials place thorns on Jesus' head and tease him.

The carrying of the cross: Jesus struggles with the heavy wood.

The crucifixion: Jesus dies on the cross.

The Luminous Mysteries – prayed on Thursdays

The baptism of Jesus: John baptizes his cousin and savior in the river.

The wedding feast at Cana: Jesus changes water into wine.

The coming of the kingdom: Jesus preaches about the kingdom of God.

The transfiguration: Jesus' appearance changes to a bright light, and God says, "This is my Son."

The Eucharist: Jesus tells us he will give us his body and blood at the Last Supper.

The Glorious Mysteries – prayed on Wednesdays and Sundays

The resurrection: Jesus rises from the dead.

The ascension of the Lord: Jesus is lifted into heaven.

The descent of the Holy Spirit: Jesus sends his Spirit to help the apostles spread God's word.

The assumption of our Blessed Mother: Mary is taken, body and soul, into heaven.

The crowning of Mary as Queen of Heaven: She wears a crown of twelve stars.

HAIL, HOLY QUEEN

Hail, Holy Queen, Mother of Mercy.
Hail, our life, our sweetness, and our hope.
To you do we cry, poor banished children of Eve.
To you do we send up our sighs, mourning and weeping
in this vale of tears.
Turn then, most gracious advocate, your eyes of mercy
toward us,
and after this, our exile,
show unto us the blessed fruit of your womb, Jesus.
O clement, O loving, O sweet Virgin Mary.

R. Pray for us, O holy Mother of God,
V. that we may be made worthy of the promises of Christ.

Let us pray:
O God, whose only begotten Son,
by his life, death, and resurrection,
has purchased for us the rewards of eternal life,
grant, we beseech you,
that meditating upon these mysteries
in the most holy Rosary of the Blessed Virgin Mary,
we may both imitate what they contain,
and obtain what they promise.
Through the same Christ our Lord.
Amen.

Even When Your Mom on Earth ...

Even when your mom on earth is busy,
making dinner and answering the phone
and folding the laundry and feeding the dog,
your mother in heaven has time.
Mary is listening.

Even when your mom on earth is grouchy,
stuck in traffic and late for your soccer practice
and tired from work and ready to go home,
your mother in heaven is peaceful.
Mary is offering her grace.

Even when your mom on earth is mad,
because you punched your friend and spilled your milk
and forgot your homework and whined,
your mother in heaven is gentle.
Mary loves you.

And when your mom on earth is happy,
kissing you, hugging you, playing with you,
holding you close to her heart,
your mother in heaven is smiling.
Mary knows the heartache and joy of being a mother,
and Mary loves your mom, too.

Dearest Mother in heaven,
hear us and grant us your peace, grace, joy, and love.
Inspire us, help us, give us hope.
Share with all God's children the gentle care you
bestowed upon your Son, Jesus. Amen.

WHEN THE SPIRIT MOVES ME

Prayers to the Holy Spirit

Come, Holy Spirit (*Veni Creator*)

Come, Holy Spirit, fill the hearts of your faithful
and enkindle in them the fire of your love.
Send forth your Spirit and they shall be created,
and you shall renew the face of the earth.

O God, who does instruct the hearts of the faithful
by the light of the Holy Spirit, grant us by the same Holy
Spirit a love and relish of what is right and just and a con-
stant enjoyment of his comforts, through Christ our Lord.
Amen.

Prayer to the Holy Spirit

Breathe into me, Holy Spirit, that my thoughts may all be
holy. Move in me, Holy Spirit, that my work, too, may be
holy. Attract my heart, Holy Spirit, that I may love only
what is holy. Strengthen me, Holy Spirit, that I may
defend all that is holy. Protect me, Holy Spirit, that
I may always be holy. Amen.

— By Saint Augustine

Whisper to Me, Blow Me Away

Holy Spirit come fill me, fill up my heart, fill up my mind.
Holy Spirit flow through me,
    bring blessings of every kind.
Holy Spirit come from me, come from my words,
    come from my deeds.
Holy Spirit pour out me, fulfilling your children's needs.
Holy Spirit come softly, a whisper of grace,
    shimmering light.
Holy Spirit come loudly, blow me away with your might.
Amen.

CHATTING WITH HIM ALL DAY LONG

Prayers for Every Part of the Day

MORNING OFFERING

O Jesus, through the Immaculate Heart of Mary,
I offer you my prayers, works, joys, and sufferings of this
day in union with the holy sacrifice of the Mass throughout the world. I offer them for all the intentions of your
Sacred Heart: the salvation of souls, reparation for sin,
the reunion of all Christians. I offer them for the intentions of our bishops and of all apostles of prayer, and in
particular for those recommended by our Holy Father this
month.
Amen.

MEAL PRAYER

Bless us O Lord, and these thy
gifts, which we are about to
receive from thy bounty,
through Christ our Lord.
Amen.

Now I Lay Me Down to (Try to) Sleep

Now I lie down to try to sleep,
I pray the Lord I won't make a peep.
I'm not really tired; I'd much rather play,
It's no fun to stop at the end of the day.
But since I am stuck here, going to bed,
I'll spend this time talking to you instead.
I know that you, Mom, and Dad know best,
And they told me to lie down and get some rest.

So I will listen, and I will obey,
and while I'm in here I just may,
send my prayers to you till dawn.
(If I can stop this great big YAWN...)
Amen.

GIVE ME STRENGTH

These short prayers are great to say anytime during the day ~ when you have to wait in line, when you're nervous about a test, when your friend is being rude, when you're all alone and want to feel close to Jesus. Learn a few by heart, and say one over and over when you need to call on God.

Be near me, Lord.

I will show your love.

Holy Spirit, help me.

Guide my heart, God.

Give me strength.

Jesus always loves me.

Father, I will follow you.

Give it to God.

Peace, please.

I NEED A HAND, GOD

Prayers of Petition and Intercession

The Sacrament of Reconciliation – Going to Confession

It can be really hard – sometimes even embarrassing – to admit when you've done something wrong and to say you are sorry. But sin pushes you away from God. Like a good shepherd looking for his lost sheep, God looks for you and wants you to be close to him. He gives you the sacrament of reconciliation as a way to get rid of that sin, to say you are sorry, and to be a part of his flock of believers again. Confessing your sins, making up for the things you did wrong, and promising to try to do better all make God happy – and make you feel great, too.

1. First spend some time thinking about the things you've done wrong.

2. Next go to a priest, who is able to deliver God's forgiveness.

3. Make the Sign of the Cross and say to the priest: "Bless me, Father, for I have sinned." Tell him how long it has been since your last confession.

4. The priest then may read from the Bible. When he pauses and asks you to confess your sins, tell him everything that's on your mind. Don't be scared – the priest will respond with God's love and mercy.

5. After you have finished telling the priest your sins, say: "I am sorry for these and all my sins."

6. The priest will give you a penance – it might be prayers or a good deed to make up for your sins.

7. Say an Act of Contrition (see p. 41 or say your own).

8. The priest will say a prayer absolving you from (forgiving) your sins. Make the Sign of the Cross again and say "Amen."

9. The priest will finish with a prayer such as "Give thanks to the Lord for he is good." You should say: "His mercy endures forever." With that, you are free of your sins! You may leave quietly to do your penance.

ACTS OF CONTRITION

O my God,
I am sorry for my sins with all my heart,
because by sinning I have deserved your punishment;
but, much more, I am sorry because I have offended you,
who are infinitely good and worthy to be loved
above all things.
With your help, I intend never to offend you again
and to avoid whatever leads me to sin.
Lord, have mercy and forgive me.
Amen.

Dear Jesus,
your suffering on the cross made possible
the forgiveness of the sins I confess today.
Please accept my sorrow,
and send your Holy Spirit to offer me the strength
to live as you wish me to,
in your light and grace.
Amen.

Prayer for the People in My Life

Almighty Father, please grant the people in my life
your care and protection. I ask you:
for those who are sick, healing and health;
for those who are sad, hope and happiness;
for those who are worried, strength and peace;
for those who are unkind, your light and mercy;
for those who are angry, grace and love.
Remember these special people, *(name each one)*, in your
blessings, as I remember them in my intercessions.
Amen.

Prayer Before a Big Day at School

May my mind be sharp, my hands be ready,
my answers be accurate, and my heart be at peace.
May God be with me, and share his power with me today.
Amen.

More Than Flowers and Birds

It's easy to feel worried when things go wrong, and you can't do anything to make them right. But as bad as things may seem sometimes, Jesus assures us that he has a plan. We simply need to trust him and his love for us. In the Bible verses below, Jesus shows us how God feeds the birds and helps flowers grow, even though they never work or worry. We are much more important than birds or flowers, he says, so God will give us all this and so much more. Read and think about Jesus' words when you feel anxious and don't know where to turn.

"Look at the birds of the air: they neither sow nor reap nor gather into barns, and yet your heavenly Father feeds them. Are you not of more value than they? …

"And why are you anxious about clothing? Consider the lilies of the field, how they grow; they neither toil nor spin; yet I tell you, even Solomon in all his glory was not arrayed like one of these. But if God so clothes the grass of the field, which today is alive and tomorrow is thrown into the oven, will he not much more clothe you? …

"Therefore do not be anxious about tomorrow, for tomorrow will be anxious for itself. Let the day's own trouble be sufficient for the day."
– Matthew 6:26, 28-30, 34

But God Knows

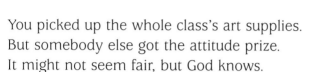

Your best friend really spilled the puzzle.
But your teacher said you were in trouble.
It might not seem fair, but God knows.

You picked up the whole class's art supplies.
But somebody else got the attitude prize.
It might not seem fair, but God knows.

Wrecking your bike was an accident.
But your dad said you had to help pay for it.
It might not seem fair, but God knows.

There's no need to argue about what's right.
Good and bad are all in God's sight.
When you do a good deed, God knows.

And if your day has you feeling down,
there's no need to walk with a frown.
When times are hard, God knows.

So try not to brag and try not to pout.
Trust in God to even things out.
Because in the end, God knows.
– Based on Matthew 6:1, 16-18

VIII.

GOD, YOU ARE SO AWESOME!

Psalms of Praise

Psalm 27

The Lord is my light and my salvation;
whom shall I fear?
The Lord is the stronghold of my life;
of whom shall I be afraid?
Though a host encamp against me,
my heart shall not fear;
though war arise against me,
yet I will be confident.
And now my head shall be lifted up
above my enemies round about me;
and I will offer ... shouts of joy;
I will sing and make melody to the Lord.

– Psalm 27:1, 3, 6

46

PSALM 147

Praise the LORD!
He heals the brokenhearted,
and binds up their wounds.
He determines the number of the stars,
he gives to all of them their names.
Great is our LORD, and abundant in power;
his understanding is beyond measure.

– Psalm 147:1, 3-5

47

PSALM 148

Praise the LORD!
Praise the LORD from the heavens,
praise him in the heights!
Praise him, all his angels,
praise him, all his host!
Praise him, sun and moon,
praise him, all you shining stars!
Praise him, you highest heavens, and
    you waters above the heavens!
Praise the LORD from the earth,
you sea monsters and all deeps,
fire and hail, snow and frost,
stormy wind fulfilling his command!
Mountains and all hills,
fruit trees and all cedars!
Beasts and all cattle,
creeping things and flying birds!
Kings of the earth and all peoples,
princes and all rulers of the earth!
Young men and maidens together,
old men and children!
Let them praise the name of the LORD,
for his name alone is exalted;
his glory is above earth and heaven.

– Psalm 148:1-4, 7-13

48

IX.

SENDING
THANK-YOU NOTES

Psalms and Prayers of Thanksgiving

Psalm 147

Sing to the LORD with thanksgiving;
make melody to our God upon the lyre!
He covers the heavens with clouds,
he prepares rain for the earth,
he makes grass grow upon the hills.
He gives to the beasts their food,
and to the young ravens which cry ...
the LORD takes pleasure in those who fear him,
in those who hope in his steadfast love.

– Psalm 147:7-11

Psalm 107

O give thanks to the LORD, for he is good;
for his steadfast love endures for ever!

– Psalm 107:1

Psalm 92

It is good to give thanks to the LORD,
to sing praises to thy name, O Most High;
to declare thy steadfast love in the morning,
and thy faithfulness by night,
to the music of the lute and the harp,
to the melody of the lyre.
For thou, O LORD, hast made me glad by thy work;
at the works of thy hands I sing for joy.

– Psalm 92:1-4

Amen and Alleluia!

Today was a good day, in every way.
Today was a great day, so I'd like to say:
Amen! Alleluia!
My classes went well, my friends were swell.
I behaved with God's help, so I'd like to yell:
Amen! Alleluia!

BASKING IN HIS LIGHT

Prayers of Blessing

Blessings from *Carmina Gadelica*

Traveling moorland, traveling townland,
traveling mossland long and wide,
God the Son about your feet,
Gold-bright angels at your side.

May God make safe to you each steep,
may God make open to you each pass,
may God make clear to you each road,
And may he take you in the clasp
of his own two hands.

God bless this house from roof to ground,
with love encircle it around.
God bless each window, bless each door,
Be thou our home for evermore.

Numbers 6

The Lord bless you and keep you:
The Lord make his face to shine upon you,
and be gracious to you:
The Lord lift up his countenance upon you,
and give you peace.

– Numbers 6:24-26

Birthday Blessing

May God bless (name), who today celebrates
the day he/she was born.
May God offer safety,
health, peace, laughter and love,
in the next year and always.

STUFF EVERY CATHOLIC KID SHOULD KNOW

Learning Our Faith Tradition

THE TEN COMMANDMENTS

1. I am the Lord, your God. You shall have no other gods besides me.
2. You shall not take the name of the Lord, your God, in vain.
3. Keep holy the Sabbath day.
4. Honor your father and mother.
5. You shall not kill.
6. You shall not commit adultery.
7. You shall not steal.
8. You shall not bear false witness against your neighbor.
9. You shall not covet your neighbor's wife.
10. You shall not covet your neighbor's possessions.

THE SACRAMENTS

Baptism
Reconciliation
Eucharist
Confirmation
Holy Orders
Matrimony
Anointing of the Sick

GIFTS OF THE SPIRIT

Wisdom
Understanding
Knowledge
Counsel
Fortitude
Piety
Fear of the Lord

Fruits of the Spirit

Charity
Joy
Peace
Patience
Kindness
Goodness
Generosity
Gentleness
Faithfulness
Modesty
Self-control
Chastity

Corporal Works of Mercy

To feed the hungry
To give drink to the thirsty
To shelter the homeless
To clothe the naked
To visit the sick
To visit those imprisoned
To bury the dead

Spiritual Works of Mercy

To admonish the sinner
To teach the ignorant
To counsel the doubtful
To comfort the sorrowful
To bear wrongs patiently
To forgive all injuries
To pray for the living and the dead

Stations of the Cross

Jesus is condemned to death.
Jesus accepts his cross.
Jesus falls.
Jesus meets his mother.
Simon takes the cross.
Veronica wipes the face of Jesus.
Jesus falls again.
Jesus meets the women.
Jesus falls the third and last time.
Jesus is stripped of his clothes.
Jesus is nailed to the cross.
Jesus dies.
Jesus is removed from the cross.
Jesus is buried.

Beatitudes

1. Blessed are the poor in spirit, for theirs is the kingdom of heaven.
2. Blessed are those who mourn, for they shall be comforted.
3. Blessed are the meek, for they shall inherit the earth.
4. Blessed are those who hunger and thirst for righteousness, for they shall be satisfied.
5. Blessed are the merciful, for they shall obtain mercy
6. Blessed are the pure in heart, for they shall see God.
7. Blessed are the peacemakers, for they shall be called sons of God.
8. Blessed are those who are persecuted for righteousness' sak for theirs is the kingdom of heaven.
9. Blessed are you when men revile you and persecute you and utter all kinds of evil agaist you falsely on my account. Rejoice and be glad, for your reward is great in heaven.

— Matthew 5:3-12

SAID ON SUNDAY

Prayers from the Mass

Each Mass has two major parts: the Liturgy of the Word and the Liturgy of the Eucharist. The Liturgy of the Word includes the Scripture readings, the Word of God. The Liturgy of the Eucharist is when we celebrate Jesus' Last Supper with his apostles, and the bread and wine become the body and blood of Christ, through the ministry of the priest.

At Mass we come together as a community to worship God. The prayers that follow are used in most Masses, either spoken or sung. By learning them you can be a part of the Mass, joining the rest of the Church in a tradition handed down over centuries.

In the name of the Father, and of the Son, and of the Holy Spirit.
Amen.

CONFITEOR

I confess to almighty God,
and to you, my brothers and sisters,
that I have sinned through my own fault
in my thoughts and in my words,
in what I have done,
and in what I have failed to do;
and I ask blessed Mary, ever virgin,
all the angels and saints,
and you, my brothers and sisters,
to pray for me to the Lord our God.

May almighty God have mercy on us,
forgive us our sins,
and bring us to everlasting life.
Amen.

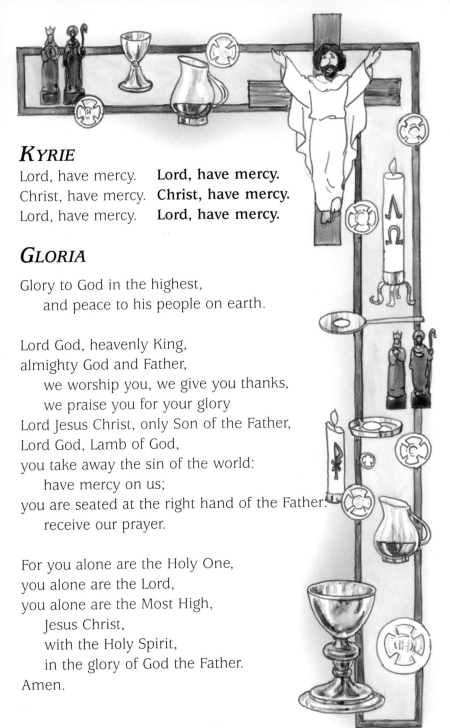

KYRIE

Lord, have mercy.	**Lord, have mercy.**
Christ, have mercy.	**Christ, have mercy.**
Lord, have mercy.	**Lord, have mercy.**

GLORIA

Glory to God in the highest,
    and peace to his people on earth.

Lord God, heavenly King,
almighty God and Father,
    we worship you, we give you thanks,
    we praise you for your glory
Lord Jesus Christ, only Son of the Father,
Lord God, Lamb of God,
you take away the sin of the world:
    have mercy on us;
you are seated at the right hand of the Father:
    receive our prayer.

For you alone are the Holy One,
you alone are the Lord,
you alone are the Most High,
    Jesus Christ,
    with the Holy Spirit,
    in the glory of God the Father.
Amen.

NICENE CREED

We believe in one God,
    the Father, the Almighty,
    maker of heaven and earth,
    of all that is seen and unseen.
We believe in one Lord, Jesus Christ,
    the only Son of God,
    eternally begotten of the Father,
    God from God, Light from Light,
    true God from true God,
    begotten, not made, one in Being with the Father.
    Through him all things were made.
    For us men and for our salvation
    he came down from heaven:
    by the power of the Holy Spirit
    he was born of the Virgin Mary,
    and became man.
    For our sake he was crucified under Pontius Pilate;
    he suffered, died, and was buried.
    On the third day he rose again
    in fulfillment of the Scriptures;
        he ascended into heaven
        and is seated at the right hand of the Father.
    He will come again in glory to judge the living and the
        dead,
    and his kingdom will have no end.
We believe in the Holy Spirit, the Lord, the giver of life,
    who proceeds from the Father and the Son.
    With the Father and the Son he is worshiped and
        glorified.
    He has spoken through the Prophets.

We believe in one holy catholic and apostolic Church.
We acknowledge one baptism for the forgiveness
of sins.
We look for the resurrection of the dead,
and the life of the world to come. Amen.

THE *SANCTUS*

Holy, holy, holy Lord, God of power and might,
heaven and earth are full of your glory.
Hosanna in the highest.
Blessed is he who comes in the name of the Lord.
Hosanna in the highest.

LAMB OF GOD

Lamb of God, you take away the sins of the
world:
have mercy on us.
Lamb of God, you take away the sins of the
world:
have mercy on us.
Lamb of God, you take away the sins of the
world:
grant us peace.

RECEIVING COMMUNION

This is the Lamb of God
who takes away the sins of the world.
Happy are those who are called to his supper.
Lord, I am not worthy to receive you,
but only say the word and I shall be healed.

The Body of Christ. **Amen.**
The Blood of Christ. **Amen.**

FINAL BLESSING

The Lord be with you.
And also with you.

May almighty God bless you,
the Father, and the Son, and the Holy Spirit.
Amen.

The Mass is ended, go in peace.
Thanks be to God.

DIVINELY INSPIRED

Notes to and from God

So What I'm Trying to Say…

The Catholic faith has many wonderful prayers, handed down year after year, century after century. But sometimes you might have a special need in your heart, a really important message for God so unique to you that no prayer you've heard seems to fit quite right. Other times you might want to pray right there on the spot, but you can't remember any particular prayer to say. At these times – or any time – you can turn your thoughts to God and simply talk to him, like the loving Father and friend he is. Jot down some of those thoughts, those conversations, those prayers in your own words that you want to recall and use again. Writing prayers is another way to demonstrate your love for Jesus. And who knows – maybe your prayer will be handed down year after year, century after century…

God Talks Back

Another important part of prayer is listening. After all, you aren't the only one with something to say. God has so much wisdom, so many lessons, so much love to share with us, if only we tune out the rest of the world and open our minds and hearts to his message. God waited for the quiet of night to whisper to Samuel, who thought it was his teacher Eli calling him at first (1 Samuel 3). God had to do more to get the attention of Saint Paul – he struck Paul with lightning, according to Tradition, as Paul rode to Damascus, knocking him off his horse and blinding him. Paul became one of Jesus' greatest disciples (Acts 9). Write what you hear when you listen to God with your mind and your heart, whether it's a shout from above or a whisper in the dark.